FROM DEATH
To Life

Rescued from Suicide's Grip

FROM DEATH
To Life

Rescued from Suicide's Grip

MARLENE E. KELLY

GreenTree Publishers
Newnan, Georgia

From Death to Life: Rescued from Suicide's Grip
Copyright © 2017 by Marlene Kelly

Unless otherwise noted, Scripture is taken from the *The Holy Bible, King James Version*. Cambridge Edition: 1769

Vector graphics were created by Asmaarzq - Freepik.com
Cover Design by Jennifer Riggs - .jenniferriggs.com

Printed in the United States of America
ISBN-13: 978-1-944483-11-1 (GreenTree Publishers)
ISBN-10: 1-944483-11-X

GreenTree Publishers
www.greentreepublishers.com

ACKNOWLEDGMENTS

I am greatly indebted to my children, my family, and my friends for all of their positive input into my life. I especially want to thank Jan Olden for her patient help in reading this manuscript to make it excel. And to my excellent copy editor, Edwina Cowgill, who tied it all together.

DEDICATION

To the millions of people who think suicide is the answer, may you all find the God of life!

TABLE OF CONTENTS

Chapter I
My Awakening

"We mothers that have buried our children, move through the shadows of life wrapped in our mourning shawls never quite fitting into the woven tapestry of society, for we are our own society born out of grief and pain in the heart." Unknown Author

A cold chill gripped my body as I feebly maneuvered through a maze of corridors leading to the body identification room in the county morgue. Inside, the room was ice cold. My eyes travelled towards the motionless body of my son lying on a metal slab. Gasping, I gripped my chest trying to stop the rapid pounding of my heart. The police officer escorted me to the slab, and I stared into a bloody, distorted face that I tried to believe wasn't my son; but it was. I reached out to wipe the blood away from his hair and face but the coroner grabbed my hand and shook his head at me *No, no!* And I was quickly escorted out of the room.

My son was shot several times in his head and left to die on a desolate, dark street in Los Angeles, California. The horror of his murder drastically altered my vision and my purpose for living. All my hopes disappeared, and all my dreams died at the exact moment breath left his body. I wanted to go to the grave with him because I didn't want him to make that transition alone. For days that led into weeks I cried and moaned, "My magnificent, wonderful son is gone; the strength of my life is gone. Why me? How could this happen to me? Why now? Why my loved one? Why not me? How could I have prevented this?" I wailed on and on.

Those questions, spawned by self-pity and self-centeredness, were statements brought on partly by the guilt of being a single mom and not being able to give my children enough of me, enough of life, and enough material possessions. I considered myself a failure. My thoughts became my tormentors.

After days of wallowing in grief, I recalled a passage from a bestselling psychology book that I read years ago, which stated, "Anguish of the mind has driven thousands to suicide; anguish of body, none. This proves that the health of the mind is of far more consequence to our happiness than the health of the body, although both deserve much more attention than either of them receives."

My attention focused on the word "suicide." That word flashed back and forth in my mind like a neon sign. Since I never grasped an understanding of how to really live without my children, or my family, it was easy to give suicide a consideration.

Finally, in my confused, troubled mind I reasoned, "My only answer to removing this pain in my heart is suicide—the great escape. Then, I can join my son. My death will be the best thing for all involved. I'm tired; I'm a failure as a wife and mother. In death, my struggles will finally be over."

Before I could change my mind, I hurriedly gulped a handful of sleeping pills and pain pills and chased them down with a can of beer. I crawled into bed and calmly laid and waited for "death" to visit me.

"I'll soon be with my wonderful son again," I moaned as I gradually drifted off to sleep.

Moments later in my mind, I envisioned a long, wide tunnel opening with the far end leading out to an ocean. Next, I saw myself running to the edge of the tunnel, jumping into the water and climbing onto a bobbing ocean wave, which I rode way out to the middle of the dark sea.

"Peace, sweet peace," I mumbled as I sank into an unconscious condition.

Suddenly, I was aware of being tossed to and fro on the wave accompanied by an intrusive persistent shaking of my body. It was the paramedics that Cassie, my dearest friend all the way through this dramatic turmoil, called when her relentless knocking at my door returned no response. Being aware of my state of mind, Cassie thought she should summon help to gain entrance. When Cassie saw my lifeless body, she was glad that she called for an ambulance.

"Wait a minute," I thought. "If I can feel, that means I'm not dead."

I struggled to open my eyes, and as I looked around, I realized I was in a hospital room, not my bedroom. I became angry and agitated that I was still alive. But before I could protest, I was hurriedly moved to another room where people, all dressed in white, were busily trying to save my life by hooking my body up to various machines and packing it in ice.

"My right to die is being violated," I snapped as I drifted back to sleep.

After what seemed an eternity, my eyes opened and squinted at several smiling faces gawking at me.

Startled and groggy, I asked, "Who are you?"

A loud voice responded to my question and proclaimed, "We are from Redeemer Church and we've come to give you some good news! God loves you."

"Read this! It will explain," another voice demanded while handing me a pamphlet.

"I don't feel like reading. I just want to be left alone to die. Please go away. My right to privacy is being violated!" I screamed.

"Will it be all right if we pray for you?" another asked.

I heard voices in my mind repeatedly saying, "You're not worthy of God's love or their prayers."

I agreed with the voices and reasoned, "I'm not pleasing to God, and He won't forgive me anyhow for trying to kill myself, so why pray?"

Besides, I was angry with God that I was still alive, so I sarcastically replied, "I don't care. Sure, pray and then leave me alone."

Their prayers for me to be forgiven and redeemed calmed me a little, but I was still shaking from the trauma of being revived. Escaping from the jaws of death was far more painful than dying. I managed to express my agony with a chilling scream, and everyone in the room scattered except my nurse. She stuck me with a needle that injected a sedative into my body that was so strong it instantly knocked me out. That battle lasted for days.

Before my release from the hospital, I was ordered to speak to a counselor. It was a mandatory procedure for all attempted suicides. I did not look forward to re-hashing all the events of my life with a stranger. But ready or not, there he was standing at the doorway of my room dressed in white (the standard garb of the hospital) with a warm inviting smile on his ruddy face.

"Good morning; I'm Jeff," he said in a soothing tone. "I'm here to help you sort out your future plans."

I laughed and replied, "What future?"

"Yours—you have a brand new one now."

I looked at him in disbelief, but I had no choice if I wanted to be released to go home and not to an institution. I had to go along with the program and submit to counseling. However, after weeks of daily counseling sessions with Jeff, I discovered that I let my ignorance, and the words of the "mind expert," one of the world's leading psychoanalysts, trick me into believing that suicide solves everything.

Jeff explained, "Death is a natural fact of life. All who come into this world must experience it at some time or another. When grief strikes your heart with its thunderous blow it leaves denial in the wound; denial that the incident happened and disbelief that the incident could happen to your loved one. Afterwards, when acceptance finally settles in, anger rises up to take the place that denial occupied. Then anger and helplessness take over as roommates and begin to play vicious tricks on your mind such as 'suicide is the answer.' Anger and hatred always produce self-destruction. The angry reaction will only lead you down the path of hatred and bitterness. If they are not addressed, you will one day find yourself full of all kinds of sicknesses, diseases, and finally death. The medical profession has proven that these reactions will produce negative symptoms to fester and grow into unwanted diseases, such as cancer, that eventually lead to death."

"How wise he is," I thought.

In another one of our sessions, Jeff explained that he was a born again Christian. He began to tell me about life being a precious gift from God.

I never looked at life in that way before.

"Suicide is not an alternative choice for relieving life's pain and suffering," explained Jeff. "In fact, it creates more pain and hardship for the survivor."

I reluctantly agreed with that insight. "I'm suffering more now than before, considering the many needle punctures in my arms and the tubes that were shoved down my throat in order to revive me," I replied.

"Well, consider the pain and suffering your savior, Jesus, went through to purchase eternal life for you," Jeff replied.

I began to cry at the thought of my shame. However, Jeff continued to console me with words he memorized from Scripture. For example:

"For God so loved the world that He gave His only begotten Son, that whosoever believeth in Him should not perish, but have everlasting life" (John 3:16).

And, "I am the way, the truth, and the life: no man cometh unto the Father, but by Me" (John 14:6).

Eventually, I desired to hear more and more of God's Word. I looked forward to all of my sessions with Jeff, up until the day I was discharged from the hospital.

Food for Thought…

There is an art to living. On one canvas is painted a sign: *Do not listen to voices that lead you to destruction and death*. Deception has caused many souls to take the wrong path to try to solve what seemed to be an unsurmountable problem.

- Can you recall a time when seemingly good advice turned bad?
- Do you remember when a seemingly good friend led you to make a wrong turn?
- How do you discern the right way to take when you have multiple options?
- How would the words of Psalms 119:105 relate to the challenge of choosing the right path for your life?

Thy word is a lamp unto my feet
And a light unto my path.   Psalm 119:105

This is me and my son on his college graduation day approximately three weeks before his death.

CHAPTER II
The Quest

"And you will seek Me and find Me when you search for Me with all your heart." Jeremiah 29:13

Upon returning home from the hospital, I strongly desired more help to mend the frayed pieces of my mind. I wanted to stop thinking about the parts of my flawed memory that didn't make sense. I craved inner peace; however, I didn't know where to go or which way to turn to find it. Jeff tried to tell me, but I couldn't grasp hold of everything he taught me. I knew that I felt a tranquil sense of peace in those sessions that made me want more. Some of my concerned and spiritually aware friends advised me that only God can give peace and a new direction. I was eager and ready to listen to their advice. So for many weeks, I allowed them to share with me their travelled paths toward spiritual enlightenment.

First, we visited a Unity church. But, the agape love, gospel truth, and God's forgiveness that Jeff taught me, were not there, because Unity's focus is on reincarnation and mental healing along with meditation. The church dwells more on man and man's abilities than on God. Also, they reject the belief in the inspiration or absolute authority of the Bible. For example, in their statement of faith they write:

"We believe the Scriptures are the testimonials of men who have in a measure apprehended the divine Logos, but that their writings should not be taken as final."

Next, we went to a Christian Science church, which is a metaphysical religion, focused on mind salvation not on spirit salvation. This church believes in the power of positive thinking, which is meant to bring all good into your life, but "it" (what I was seeking) was not there.

Our next stop was the Transcendental Meditation Church (TM) where they believe meditation blanks out the conscious mind and focuses on self-realization or an inner light. While sitting in awkward twisted positions for hours I tried to get out of my body to find peace and God, but He was not there either.

From there we visited a Theosophical meeting, a New Age meeting, a Bahia meeting, and another metaphysics meeting. The God of Abraham, Isaac and Jacob, with the peace I was seeking, was not in any of those meetings either because they all believed in an impersonal god that one senses and feels for universal energy, or they worshiped the philosophies of man.

Eventually, I became frustrated with all the confusion coming from their elusive search. Not long after, I moved to San Francisco and my friends and I parted ways. I started a new search on my own, which led me to become involved with the Haight/Ashbury Hippie revolution that was extremely popular at that time. That movement incorporated belief in and practice of numerology, astrology, the power of positive thinking philosophy, and horoscopes. This was a natural for me to pick up because my grandmother would never leave home until she had read her horoscope for the day. In addition, marijuana and alcohol were now my daily food. Of course, I didn't find God or inner peace in any of those excursions. On the contrary, I was descending back downward into darkness.

Many weeks later, my journey led me to visit an occult bookstore where I was trying to find more literature on the supernatural. A flyer tacked on a wall behind the cashier announced that they held séances in one of the many rooms. While I was engrossed in reading the information on the flyer, the cashier invited me to attend a séance. I thought it would be a perfect opportunity to try to contact my deceased son, so I accepted the invitation.

The night of the séance, I sat in a circle with other lost souls trying to call up spirits. I focused on calling the spirit of my deceased son. The experience was like being in a dream, like seeing it at a movie, like leaving my body and watching from the outside. After what seemed like hours, I had a sudden urge to leave. At that time, I really couldn't discern where the feeling to run was coming from; my spirit hadn't been renewed enough to know good from that kind of evil. But I sensed what I was doing was wrong. I thought calling up dead spirits, or familiar spirits, was a good thing. Nevertheless, I felt so horribly uncomfortable in my skin that I never attended another session or went near that bookstore again.

I later discovered that occult practice is called "Spiritism." That experience in the occult bookstore

was so frightening, coupled with such a strong presence of evil in the room, I became inundated with
more fear and depression. For weeks after that forbid-
den experience and my association with those people,
I was frequently visited in the night by haunting nightmares, such as a scarred, twisted, tortured face covered
in blood screaming curses at me. I could never fully
understand the words but it felt as though Satan, my
adversary, was trying to claim my life once again with
dreams and thoughts of self-destruction. But Father
God had a plan for my life that was greater than what
the devil planned for me. Praise God!

Still in search of a new direction for my mind and
my life, I heeded the urging of my friend and enrolled
at the local university where I began attending classes
in Philosophy and Psychology. I wanted to learn more
about religion, the Bible and also the inner workings
of the mind. I believed I would find all the answers to
the many questions I had in books and not from tele-
vision. For example, I learned in one of the classes that
the occult has been around since the great civilizations
of Babylon, Egypt, Greece, and Rome. I discovered
that most of the occult practices encompass idolatry
and false religions. Also, dabbling in the occult brings
bondage to sin, darkness to the soul, and estrangement
from God and His word. It causes a person to rebel,

and be oppressed by evil spirits (demons), which promotes mental and emotional disturbances such as depression, neuroses, oppression, and suicidal thoughts.

"Wow!" I exclaimed, "That is exactly what happened to me."

I reasoned, "Once those tormenting thoughts were accepted and acted on, my mind was out of control. Satan is a master mind controller."

"Thus saith the LORD GOD; It shall come to pass, that at the same time shall things come into thy mind, and thou shalt think an evil thought" (Ezekiel 38:10). Yet, at the time, I did not connect this new-found information to my past suicide attempt.

During fall registration for classes, I was handed a flyer announcing the formation of a new Bible study to be held in a nearby classroom. I decided to go and see if I could get some relief from the nagging heaviness in my soul. Father God, The Lord Jesus Christ, and the Holy Spirit met me inside that classroom.

My human incompleteness met divine completeness, and I was filled and made whole. What was lacking in the churches I visited, I found in that classroom Bible study, and I have never been the same, nor have I ever wanted to be. I was able to see, hear, and realize that God had a plan for my life other than death. As a result, I surrendered my will to God's will, and thus became a born-again Christian, which meant I gave Jesus Christ control over my life. I surrendered my will unto His and became whole and at peace for the first time in my life. I looked at the world with a new vision, a new compassion for mankind. I wanted to tell everyone how to be made free.

"How sweet it is to be free," I sang as I danced, twirled, and skipped through the campus to the parking lot.

"The chains of sin are broken," I cried. "Grief is gone, joy has replaced it; darkness is gone, light has replaced it; and occult bondages are broken, freedom in Christ has replaced it."

The winds of sorrow passed over me, allowing the warm rays from the sun to kiss my face and dry all my tears. Jesus Christ will always bring peace to a raging storm entwined within a human soul. The Holy Spirit moves into secret hidden rooms in your mind that were padlocked for years and gently sweeps away the cobwebs. He lets in the Light of salvation and deliverance to restore you to a new creation in Christ Jesus and sets you free from the bondage of spiritual ignorance. I realized that God does not cause the storms, but He allows them for His purpose and His glory in my life. Father God wants to improve me in the midst of my storms before He removes them.

Later that night in the quiet confines of my room while I was meditating on my new experience, I finally read the Gospel pamphlet that those Christians at the hospital were trying to urge me to read.

"I know the thoughts that I think toward you," says the LORD, "thoughts of peace, and not of evil, to give you an expected end." Jeremiah 29:11 (KJV)

"That's it!" I sighed. "I was brainwashed into believing that death was better than life; that my life had no purpose; that I was alone, unloved and worthless. But God promises in His word to provide the wisdom and discernment needed to uncover and disarm every destructive device evil has placed along my path."

And He did. I spent almost a year repenting of all the sins I committed by being in agreement with the occult (Leviticus 19:31) and any other ungodly practices.

"How stupid I was to believe the lies of the enemy," I confessed. "Look what I would've missed."

Food for Thought...

Have you ever asked yourself this question: Is this all there is to life? Or why am I here on this planet? Sometimes we feel like our lives are meaningless and have no purpose. Only God can fill your emptiness and give you everlasting peace and joy.

- Do you have trouble with understanding God's purpose for your life?

- When was the last time you were disappointed with yourself and/or with others? What was your conclusion?

- Can you connect your life to a bigger mission that God has for you?

- The Apostle Paul struggled with understanding his purpose in life until he met Christ. Read Philippians 3:4-14 and note Paul's conclusions.

That I may know Him, and the power
of His resurrection, and the fellowship
of His sufferings; being made
conformable to His death. Philippians 3:10

I was saved less than a week when this picture was taken.

I attended this mission as a young believer.

CHAPTER III
Faith Walk

I don't see the problem; I see only
   The promise
I'm not looking to go under, but to go over.
Faith is not built in comfortable places!
Faith gives me the vision!
Faith is trusting in God not self.
(Excerpt from a sermon on faith)
   Numbers 9:17-23 & Deut. 8:2

Having received the precious gift of God's salvation in my late 30's gave me a new exciting life with Christ, but the joy of my new experience caused me to

look sorrowfully back at my wasted years of commit-
ting sin and causing grief. However, Father God gave
me a Comforter (The Holy Spirit) to bind up my
wounds from the past. His perfect remedy for all the
remorseful "pity-party" stuff was for me to receive
more freedom from condemnation by attending a
Christian retreat center in the beautiful California San
Gabriel Mountains.

The retreat center was a heavenly place wrapped in
a cloud of peace and perfection, set-aside especially for
God's children to commune with Him and rest. It was
a holy place, bathed in prayer where one could find
answers and increase in faith. It was surrounded by
majestic mountains, tranquil waterfalls, and colorful
singing birds nested in stately trees whose branches
fanned the warm breath of summer winds. The deli-
cate fragrance emitting from the many yellow daffodils
pointing their orange centers toward huge sunflowers,
which lined the path to the main building, sent a
breathtaking aroma in the air. At special times, I
glimpsed from the bus window nature's gentle animals
peeking back toward me from the corner of their eyes.

"This must be what the Garden of Eden was like."
I imagined.

"God is so good!" I thought. "I never want to
leave this place," I cried, looking up to heaven.

Then I heard my thoughts. "Of course not! I feel safe and secure here, but when the time comes, I have to go down the mountain into the chaotic world below." I suddenly felt chilled and I shuddered at the thought of leaving.

"We're almost there, folks," said the bus driver, Annie, a sweet gentle spirit. She was singing all the way up the mountain. Later I found out she was happy because she was escaping from an abusive husband and three unruly spoiled kids for the duration of this retreat. For the first time in 10 years, she was alone and away from them.

"You are so blessed to have a family," Carol said to Annie. She was a new Christian and extremely lonely and shy. It was amazing that she spoke up to say anything.

Annie replied jokingly, "Yea, well I guess they beat a blank."

I interpreted her statement to mean that having her children was better than not having a family at all. From the expression on Carol's face, she did not see the humor in Annie's remark. I sensed an uninvited guest called "tension" beginning to invade the atmosphere so, I began singing the hymn *Amazing Grace,* and every one joined in.

Finally, after what seemed like many grueling hours, the bus pulled into the retreat campground parking lot. A gleeful cheer went out from all of us, and a grateful applause for Annie.

Weary from the trip but anxious to see what Father God was going to do, I flopped down on the bed in my room, closed my eyes, and began to meditate on the goodness of God and all of His mercies. My room-mate soon arrived with all her suitcases, so I had to get up and make a way for her to share our closet.

"Hi! My name is Ella," she said with a sweet angelic tone of voice.

Walking toward her with my arms outstretched, I gave her a hug as I introduced myself.

"I needed that," she said. "I'm so nervous because this is my first retreat."

"Mine too," I reassured her.

A knock on the door announcing that lunch was being served in the dining hall interrupted our get acquainted conversation.

Afterwards, we were blessed with a message from the retreat pastor about what was expected from us and what we could expect from God.

"If my people, which are called by my name will humble themselves, and pray, and seek my face, and turn from their wicked ways; then will I hear from heaven, and will forgive their sin, and will heal their land." 2 Chronicles 7:14 was the foundational scripture.

The message pierced my heart and brought tears to my eyes as I reflected on the price that Jesus paid to redeem me from a life of sin. I had never experienced such unselfish love before Jesus Christ. And to think that all He wanted from me was my love and obedience, my belief and trust. I cried, repented and prayed for forgiveness that night until I was blessed with sweet refreshing sleep.

Early the next morning I had at least three hours of personal time of prayer and meditation. I decided to spend the time in the towering mountains that surrounded the center, hiking as far as I could endure the climb. At the top of a huge canyon, I stopped to rest. A large rock served as a perch from which I gazed across the surrounding mountains awe struck, amazed, and fascinated by God's magnificent handiwork. He carved each mountain just so precisely, that the formation of layers of rock fitted into other layers of rock to eventually form those huge grand magnificent mountains.

Suddenly, I understood, with the help of the precious Holy Spirit, that in the same way the layers of rock fit into other layers of rock to form a mountain, unconfessed sin piles up on top of unconfessed sin and weighs us down in our spirits. As a result, I could never look at a mountain the same anymore.

That experience put a rising love in my heart and praise on my lips to my God for His abundant grace and goodness. It left me knowing that whatever comes my way, God, in His sovereignty, is faithful to work all things out for my good. Faith is the ability to feel so sure of God, that no matter how dark the day, there is no doubt as to the outcome. For Father God's children, there is always a glorious, successful conclusion.

"I'm so glad to be His child," I shouted as I made my way back to the retreat center.

After finishing a savory evening meal, I hurriedly entered the sanctuary for the evening message. I sat as close to the podium as possible because I didn't want to miss a word.

The minister began by saying, "The mind controlled by the Spirit, is life and peace. Therefore, you will find that inner peace when you renew your mind. The idea that we leave our mind behind when we become Christians is blatantly unbiblical. Repentance means to change your mind."

"Wow! He is talking to me," I whispered to myself. *How did he know about the battles I've had with mind control?*

I sat and listened attentively throughout the entire two-hour message, occasionally wiping tears from my eyes.

"Now roll all your evil thoughts in a bag; throw them down on the floor and stomp on them! Do it now! Get up on your feet and stomp," the minister said.

It felt strange, but I obeyed. As I was stomping, I felt a release in my spirit followed by a "peace that passes all understanding." All I could say was "Hallelujah!"

Later that night I came across this scripture Job 14:17, "My transgression is sealed up in a bag, and thou sewest up mine iniquity."

I concluded that this is what the minister was referring to. *Awesome.*

Food for Thought...

Do you find it hard to trust? Faith is trusting God and His Word. Faith believes that only God can rescue you, protect you and make you whole.

- Why do you think some people have a hard time trusting other people or even God?
- When was the last time you used faith?

- Can you think of a time you felt powerless over sin, your weakness, or over your addiction?
- How does faith turn weakness into strength?
- Read about the heroes of faith in Hebrews 11.

But without faith, it impossible to please
Him: for he that cometh to God must
believe that He is and that He is a rewarder
of them that diligently seek Him.
Hebrews 11:6

CHAPTER IV

Abusive Churches

"As the hart panteth after the water brooks,
so panteth my soul after thee." Psalm 42:1

The retreat birthed in me a hunger and thirst to know more of God and His ways. I had an overwhelming desire to please Him. One thing I learned was that I had to fellowship with other believers and go to a place called *"church"* to learn more about my new Christian life with the Lord Jesus Christ. Therefore, trying to be obedient, I happily visited a highly-recommended church.

My first Sunday wasn't too productive. After the service, the pastor asked everyone to greet me. But after the greeting was over everyone hurriedly left the sanctuary except for the workers and they were too busy to notice my need for more attention. I was a new baby Christian and not used to the ways of the "church." Determined to be obedient to Father God, I continued going to church. I realized that I, too, was now one of His, like the others in the church, so I sucked in my pouting lips and began to pray for someone to become my special spiritual friend.

The next Sunday I pressed my way into the congregation with a smiling face. I felt maybe some of them had to trust me before they warmed up to me. This I could not understand at first, but later on in my spiritual walk, I learned that was all about discernment. There were others that were too "spiritual" (holier than thou), and too "important" to give me the time of day ever. When some of the members did talk to me, it seemed that I was constantly being judged by my lack of years of salvation, or what profession I was in, or what church I came from, or where did I receive my salvation, or if I was spirit filled, or if I was baptized, etc., etc. I felt as though I was still in the secular world having to present a resume with credentials.

"What's so different about being a Christian?" I asked God.

After a few months, I became disappointed and disillusioned with church and all its trappings. When I heard voices in my mind telling me to "Leave the church and Jesus and return to the secular world where you know how to play the game," I agreed.

It was at that point I felt the overwhelming presence of the Holy Ghost for the first time since I became Spirit filled. I began to talk it over with Father God and relate my hurt feelings to Him.

Then, I clearly heard God's voice say, "Who died for you on the cross?"

"Jesus," I answered.

"Who saved you from you sins?" He asked.

"Jesus," I replied.

"Who do you go to church to learn about?" He continued.

"Jesus, Jesus, Jesus," I sobbed.

"Then keep your eyes on Me and not man. Look to Me, not your brothers and sisters in church. You pray for them and leave them to Me," He commanded.

"Yes, Lord! Yes, Lord!" I cried.

It was clear that my focus must be entirely on Jesus, and I must crucify the desires of my flesh.

After that, I was content to be in solitary confinement with the Lord. I began to run the race, looking unto Jesus only, the Author and Finisher of my salvation. I realized that any real spiritual fellowship had to be ordered by Him when it was His time for that to happen. For now, I had to read the Bible to *"study to show myself approved."*

I attended as many services as my schedule would allow. I looked and listened intently to my new brethren and heard what seemed to be a strange new vocabulary: the anointing, rest in God, grace, rejoice in tribulation, new creature, new man, old man, etc. I felt like a baby learning a new language, but, to this new life, I was exactly that. I wanted to catch-up and grow up as fast as I could. I wanted to speak the new language, bask in the new lifestyle, and embrace the inner peace that came with my conversion. The more I studied and learned the Word of God, the more I wanted to know. I couldn't get enough. My thirst and my hunger were never satisfied. I knew there had to be more to come, so I prayed for more. "Deeper LORD, take me deeper."

Father God heard my prayer and answered. I quickly began to grow in the Word of God. I had to learn to wait on God's timing in all things. I was truly excited about Jesus, and so in love with Him that everything else became minimized in His light. He consumed my thoughts to the point I never experienced any nightmares again. All sorrow and confusion were gone from my mind. Everything was so clear, so pure in the light that filled my soul. How strange yet how simple it was now to completely know that Jesus was all I ever needed.

"For with thee is the fountain of life; in thy light shall we see light." (Psalm 36:9).

Slowly over the course of time, I began to meet genuine Christian people in the church. The Christians that chose to fellowship with me were seriously dedicated (sold-out) disciples of the Lord. They lived their lives by the highest standards of the Christian walk, by attempting to walk in obedience to the Word of God, imitating Jesus in all their ways. They inspired me to a higher spiritual growth. But unfortunately, I wasn't around them enough. Only two or three times a week at church wasn't enough fellowship for me. I needed to know how to conduct myself as a Christian 24 hours a day 365 days a year.

Praise God, I soon discovered that it was the job of the Holy Spirit to comfort me and fellowship with me when I was alone. He began to teach me out of the Bible and through prayer, and the Holy Spirit never tired of cleansing me. I would sit in service and cry when I heard the Word of God. I would cry when souls answered the altar call for salvation. I would cry at home, cry at work, cry in the car; I thought that I was never going to stop crying. I learned that those tears were cleansing tears for my sins.

At length, I started visiting other churches in the area until I found myself enticed by a group of Christians who were mightily involved with supernatural experiences. Some of them were very prominent in Charismatic Christian circles and enjoyed the highly sought after prophetic ministry gifts. Their church services were always a "supernatural" event. The congregation sang at times like a heavenly spiritual choir of anointed angelic voices, which often brought tears to my eyes. The pastor was extremely charismatic and would occasionally fall to his knees and pray and weep during his messages. Some members would break out in the "holy dance" and others would speak in "tongues," while still others gave the "interpretation of the tongue." It was not unusual for some members in the congregation to break out, running around the church praising God.

As one visitor put it, "This church is wild! They swing from the chandeliers and leap over chairs. Hallelujah!"

I became caught up in "not having church as usual." After attending their Bible studies, I eventually joined this church of diverse nationalities, because I felt they genuinely loved Jesus and me. They were knowledgeable of His Word and ways, which they skillfully taught. I frequently attended their very intense intercessory prayer group, where they battled in prayer with the "Spirit" for hours until break-through was achieved. On occasion, I would venture out with them to their many mountain retreats, where they offered daily prayers for the church, lost souls and many foreign countries.

After some time, I became a student in the church's prophetic ministry school. I trained to hear God's voice and speak out His Word. Being a some-what new Christian, I did not discern that this was not the way God trains you to hear from Him. I became caught up in the self-importance of giving prophetic utterances on demand while ignoring the still small voice of the Holy Spirit nudging me to realize some-thing wasn't right with this procedure. I felt as though I was being wound up and then told what and when to speak. It was as if others were controlling my mind and spirit apart from God. I began to pull back when a female church member started following me around and asking, "Give me a word from the Lord."

Someone once said, "Imitation is the sincerest form of flattery and admiration." Consequently, I began to imitate the pastors and members by practic-ing the "holy dance," the "holy look," and the "holy talk," but I gave no mercy, no charity, and no for-giveness to anyone. Many were the wounds I inflicted on others in the name of the Lord. I strutted around like a proud peacock. After all, I was chosen, highly favored and anointed, by God to do marvelous things. According to the pastor, I was God's child, His prophet, and His delivering agent.

Before I realized it, I moved from God's grace to legalism (working works instead of resting in faith). I tried to justify my place in God's family by working formulas such as, *Seven Steps to Glory*, *Twelve Steps to Holiness*, and *Five Easy Steps to Being an Over-comer*, instead of trusting and resting in the cross-saving faith of Jesus. I hung scriptures on the walls of my home, around my neck, and carried them in my wallet, which I used to enforce my claim of being holy. I began to beat people over their heads with a "holy hammer" of condemnation. People would call me the "hammer" and I would laugh, but I'm sure that Father God cried. He waited patiently for me to find the "way" back to His grace and mercy.

As a result, Father God's fiery furnace especially prepared for me was getting hotter and hotter. Finally, the Holy Spirit put a big check in my spirit when the assistant pastor contracted cancer and died. The head pastor's wife contracted cancer and died. The head pastor's rebellious children were feeding on rock music, hip-hop, and rap, and they were professing to be sexually active. Finally, the last straw was that the head pastor ran off to China with his secretary. I fled from that church like Joseph fled from Potiphar's wife, but I ran right into my fiery furnace.

Food for Thought...

The long journey from salvation to transformation begins in God's church. That is where you begin to hear God's voice, learn to pray, and learn of His promises.

- Do you believe that God still speaks today?
- Can you remember a time when you heard God's voice?
- When did you have a prayer answered?
- Which promise did God keep for you?
- Read Psalm 143:10 and consider whether or not God could answer the Psalmist's prayer if God did not speak today.

Teach me to do thy will; for thou art my God: Thy Spirit is good; lead me into the land of uprightness.
Psalm 143:10

SCHOOL OF WORLD MISSION • FULLER THEOLOGICAL SEMINARY • 2001-2002

CHAPTER V
Homeless Yet in Christ

A study in dying to self and brokenness:
"Faith is a thread
Slender and frail
Easy to tear;
Yet it can lift
The weight of a soul,
Up from despair."
Matthew Biller

Spiritual pride is a killer. By definition, pride is "the vanity of self." But it can also be self-reliance, self-dependence, self-righteousness, self-satisfaction, self-glorying, self-boasting, and self-importance all cloaked in being super holy or godly. All of those conditions give rise to haughtiness, a know-it-all attitude, and arrogance. Add to those conditions pride in spiritual knowledge and insight into God's Word, and you have the deadly combination of "spiritual pride." That's why self must be crucified on the "cross." Only Jesus is important. Only Jesus matters. This lesson I had to learn the hard way, because spiritual pride had infiltrated my soul with such magnitude, Father God was obliged to use a drastic measure to purge it from me once and for all. I became homeless.

"Yes, I'm a homeless Spirit-filled Christian," I told some residents in the Skid Row mission. "I am a four–year-old Christian, full of much revelation and the Word of God; used mightily by the Holy Spirit and Father God in many ways, yet I'm homeless," I elaborated.

Their eyes were filled with disbelief as I continued to try to explain how it happened.

"My homelessness came about partly due to injuries to my lower back, which made working on a job impossible. Couple that with numerous attacks from the enemy against my finances, which resulted in unpaid bills, and that's how I became homeless. Father God used all of these events as an opportunity to teach me some valuable life lessons."

I continued, "At first, I thought it was going to be impossible for me to survive. I fasted and prayed for days for answers. Finally, I was given an eviction notice, and I moved out of my apartment. My faith was being tested and my attitude was being adjusted. Through the reality of these events, I discovered that being kicked out of my nest taught me how to fly with Jesus" (Isaiah: 40:28-31).

My testimony was received by the residents with applause. I quickly directed their admiration back to Jesus, and away from myself.

I further explained, "I have learned that every experience and every person that Father God puts into my life is in perfect preparation for my future that only He can see. For example, the only reason I did not end up residing on the streets or at the many missions was because Father God moved on the hearts of several saints from my former "first" church. They offered me space in their homes, a humbling experience, to say the least. Because of my circumstances, these friends looked at me with "spiritual eyes" that questioned my walk with God and scrutinized my every word. They corrected me often in the name of love for my apparent lack of faith. My chastisement appeared to be their assignment. I began to understand David's cry, "and let me not fall into the hands of man" (2

Samuel 24:14). Nevertheless, I was truly grateful for their hospitality and that I escaped having to sleep in a shelter."

When I finished speaking, I humbly exited the building in the midst of numerous hugs and pats on my back from many residents. Father God will always show you His unfailing love.

From the beginning of my homeless ordeal until the end, I moved nine times. Each move produced more wear and tear on my back, my nerves, and my faith. I began to suffer from "battle fatigue" and spiritual burnout, which I couldn't afford to entertain for long. I cried out day and night for mercy. Finally, Father God heard me and moved me to my sister's house.

Food for Thought...

The lifestyle of many is homelessness, but it is not one I choose for myself. God has His own way of changing a negative behavior. Therefore, after many unheeded warnings, my Spiritual pride had to be replaced by humility.

- Was there ever a time you decided to ignore God's warnings?

- Can you name an area of rebellion to God's Word in your life?

- Read Isaiah 40:8 and consider the contrast between the grass of the field and the Word of God. What is the significance for you that God's Word stands forever?

The grass withereth, the flower fadeth: but
the word of our God shall stand forever.
Isaiah 40:8

Pictures of the pastor and new believers
at the Stripes of Healing Mission.

CHAPTER VI
Sister's House

"Rejoice not against me, O mine enemy; when I fall,
I shall arise when I sit in darkness, the LORD shall
be a light unto me." Micah 7:8

God does have a sense of humor!

"I cried out for mercy, Father God," I reminded
Him as I was moving into my sister's spare room. My
sister offered me a sparsely furnished room with only
a pallet for a bed.

My dear sister is a practicing high priestess in the
Buddhist religion. It is a highly self-focused religion.
She chants a mantra three times a day to an idol on an
altar in her living room, where she places food. At the

end of the day she placed the idol's food on the kitchen table and expected me to eat it.

I declined daily and repeatedly told her, "The Word of God forbids eating food sacrificed to idols."

She laughed at my Biblical reasons and mocked God and said, "Let your God feed you then."

Sometimes I woke up at night to find her standing over me smiling and questioning me, "Where is your God now? You are homeless and sleeping on my floor in my house that my god gave me. What is your God doing for you?" she tauntingly laughed, as if Father God had forsaken me.

She was skilled at using mind control techniques. She unknowingly was being used by Satan to try to instill into my mind doubt, fear, depression, and all of those devices that he uses. But by faith, I was able to bear my sister's insults. She did this to try to make me feel guilty and ashamed for being in her house with no money or a job. She thrived off of making me appear inferior to her and her god. Nevertheless, I knew I was being instructed and humbled by my God, so I quietly endured.

Frequently, during the many long nights in my sister's house, I awakened with the sounds of voices chanting from downstairs in her den. She had gathered some of her members to assist her in chanting for me.

I learned later that they were chanting for me to become one of them.

"How ironic!" I thought, because I was praying for my sister and her group to repent and become Christians.

In spite of all the drama, sleeping on my sister's spare bedroom floor was warmer and safer than a homeless shelter or the streets. I learned another lesson: to be content and thankful in whatever situation I found myself. I thank God for keeping me throughout that trying experience. I learned firsthand about His keeping power and His faithfulness. Without it, I might have backslid into my old ways or worse.

Not long after, Father God introduced me to the burning fire of deliverance, where pride had to bow its knees, where self had to surrender and die. I began to cry out for mercy; mercy that I never extended to anyone suddenly became a very real need to me. It was a hard lesson that I had to learn.

"Mercy, mercy. Lord, please have mercy on me!"

It was difficult for me to relate to David saying in Psalm 119:71, "It was good for me that I have been afflicted; that I might learn thy statutes."

I questioned. "How can affliction be good?"

Now I know the answer. It helps subdue the crying, whining of one's flesh and breaks open one's spirit so that the true Holy Spirit can be released for ministry. Looking back, I realize that the moment I said, "Yes" to Jesus, it seemed that my afflictions from the devil increased and have not ceased. However, I can truly say the blessings from God override the afflictions.

"Praise God for them all!"

Yet, He keeps my mind through all temptations and trials. I have no desire to die anymore; instead, I fight to live. Consequently, I now enjoy a peace that I never knew before, a sweet peace in the midst of all the turmoil. My faith in God and His promises have grown, not diminished. As a result, Father God led me to still another church not far from my sister's house. The believers there prayed for me constantly. Their prayers certainly helped me to make it through the long turbulent stay at my sister's house.

Six months later, I received a check for $50,000.00, which was back pay for my disability. I rejoiced! Father God released me to move into a small apartment of my own. This was further evidence of God's keeping power.

Food for Thought...

In the Christian experience, there will come times of division, especially in your family. God's love and mercy must be evident within both the situation and the solution.

- Were there times when forgiving someone presented a problem for you?

- Can you explain how hatred, bitterness, and unforgiveness solve problems?

- If someone sins against you and you choose not to forgive them, who ultimately hurts worse? You or the one guilty of sin? How do you think God feels about a Christian who chooses not to forgive others?

- Read Ephesians 4:29-32 and consider how God calls Christians to forgive others.

And be ye kind one to another,
tenderhearted, forgiving one another, even as
God for Christ's sake hath forgiven you.
Ephesians 4:32

This is the Campus Crusade for Christ
Arrowhead Retreat Center.

CHAPTER VII

Dark Shadows on the Soul

"...I am the light of the world: he that followeth
me shall not walk in darkness, but shall
have the light of life." John 8:12

One morning as I was rejoicing and basking in the
glory of God, praising and worshiping Him, I began
to sense the presence of a shadow standing between
my Savior and me. I prayed in the Spirit, but I couldn't
press through the barrier. I started experiencing an
overwhelming sense of desolation, abandonment,
weakness, and helplessness. I felt as though I was sink-
ing into utter darkness. The brilliant light from my
Savior was becoming dim in the cold presence of this
shadow. I struggled against it, but to no avail.

"Help," I groaned, "I'm being swallowed up by its presence."

"Help me, help me, oh, please help me!"

Then in my sub-consciousness I heard, "The Blood, the Blood of Jesus."

I began speaking to the shadow, "The Blood, The Blood of Jesus is against you. Go from me now."

Like a flash, the shadow disappeared, and again, I felt the presence of God engulfing me with His agape love.

When I questioned my pastor about that experience, he said, "You're beginning to learn about spiritual warfare. It is a never-ending fight as long as you are determined to serve Christ."

He reassured me that I would always win if I stayed anchored in Jesus and His Word. That was easy for him to say, but hard for me to always do. Many times, I found myself slipping back again into old habits or territories that I had no business being in. At those times, the overwhelming darkness would return to my soul filling me with terror, torment, sickness, and disease. Trouble would visit me from every side. It seemed that these experiences intensified every time they occurred. Ultimately, I cried out to the Lord for wisdom and understanding. I needed to know exactly what I had to do to remain free of these evil occurrences. He reminded me of the scripture verse in Ephesians six that says, "We do not wrestle against flesh and blood, but against principalities, against powers, against the rulers of darkness of this age, against spiritual hosts of wickedness in the heavenly places…"

I thank God for His mercy and grace. He provided a way of escape for me again in the form of a local deliverance ministry. Through the teaching and prayers of the knowledgeable dedicated workers in that ministry, I found out the shadow hovering over me for so long was a spirit of death urging me to commit suicide.

The spirit of death is a strong force. It was the ruler spirit over all of the other hidden spirits sent to torment me. Its ultimate goal was to kill me before God could be fully glorified in my life. I believed this to be true because the Holy Spirit brought back to my remembrance the times from infancy that this spirit had raised its ugly hand against my life. The first time was when, as a newborn, my mother was bathing me, and I slipped out of her hands and almost drowned. The second time, I was six months old when my mother found me in my crib with my head caught between the bars. As a toddler, I put my finger into an electric socket and was almost electrocuted. The fourth time, I contracted measles and a high fever that sent me to the hospital. The fifth time, when I was about 10 years old and I loved to climb trees, I fell and injured my back for life. Later during that same year, a friend of the family molested me. By the time I reached my teenage years, I had such low self-esteem that I tried to cut my wrist. Finally, the spirit of death took my first-born son violently to the grave only days after he graduated from college, giving me a supreme reason to die.

I am thankful for the prayers of those believers in the deliverance ministry. God heard their prayers and mine, and He set me free forever from that horrible spirit. Now, I live to be a witness of God's love and grace.

Food for Thought…

When we enter into battle with the enemy (devil), we must remember that the battle is God's, and the victory is ours.

- Are you aware of the tactics of the enemy?
- Have you ever heard of the term "stronghold"? What do you think it means?

- How do you battle against demonic strongholds in your life?
- Read 2 Corinthians 10:3-4. What are the *weapons of our warfare?*
- Read Ephesians 6:10-18. Imagine yourself putting on the armor of God. Would you be willing to prayerfully put on God's armor each day?

Finally, my brethren, be strong in the Lord
and in the power of his might.
Ephesians 6:10

This is a picture of me and my dearest Christian
sister, Sookie. In the picture below, we are with
her family at her husband's graduation from
Fuller Theological Seminary

CHAPTER VIII

What a Path!

"The fiery-furnace proves that Father
God cares. The heat removes the impuri-
ties and solid gold comes forth."
Job 23:10

Had I been successful in killing myself, Satan
would have robbed me of this glorious, life changing
experience with the Lord Jesus Christ. When I surrendered my life back to the Lord, I couldn't begin to
imagine the path He had formed for me to take. For
example, I finished a leadership training class at
another local church, while all the time I questioned
why I was in the class in the first place. After I finished
that training, I had a brief sojourn with an overseas
mission organization, which left me again puzzled and

wondering why. Every missionary I met had a burden for a particular country, and when I was asked what country the Lord placed on my heart, I looked bewildered.

Next, Father God led me to enroll in seminary. I was so excited to be among what I thought, at the time, were great men and women of God. Instead, after living on campus for a year, I discovered that they were all like me, trying to find their place in God's Kingdom and understand their place in His scheme of things to come. None of us were perfect and we were far from great. However, I met some beautiful Christians at the seminary and developed lasting relationships. As I look back on that experience, I realize, however, I grew in wisdom with more understanding of the Bible and prayer.

I developed a lasting relationship with Sookie, my Korean neighbor in the campus dorm. When I first met Sookie, my spirit was immediately attracted to hers, probably because she was praying almost all of the time. Sookie was from South Korea where Christians believe in praying daily in church or on top of "Prayer Mountain." Because Sookie loved to pray, she felt that Americans were very strange people who prayed very little. It troubled her to see the doors of their churches locked most of the time. Father God carefully knitted us together for several years. It was a rich fellowship, and I was sad when we lost contact with each other. However, even now from time to time, I feel prompted to pray for her, and her family, and her country. I'm sure she is praying for me.

I related to another precious family who lived in the seminary dorm: Padmini, her husband Martin, and their children. They were from India. I learned more about humility from them in the short time I was in their presence than I learned from any teachings on the subject. I'm sure they are being used mightily by Father God to bring many souls into the Kingdom.

My time spent at seminary and the mission campus allowed me to meet and fellowship with Christians from almost every nation in the world. My worldview truly expanded along with my appetite for the rich variety of delicious foods. With the help of my illustrious professors, who taught me many things about the mission field and how to witness Christ' love to different cultures, my desire to serve others grew.

From there I went on to meet some great saints in YWAM (Youth with a Mission), with whom I was able to serve alongside in ministry during the Christian Olympics outreach in California. That was a glorious, soul-saving time.

Food for Thought...

From the rising of the sun, every day is a new adventure with Jesus.

- When was the last time you stepped care-free into a new adventure?

- Can you remember a time you took a risk to move out of the shadows and venture forth into the deep, infinite possibilities of life?

- Read John 10:10. Would you describe your life as being "abundant."

The thief cometh not, but for to steal, and to kill, and to destroy: I am come that they might have life, and that they might have it more abundantly. John 10:10

CHAPTER IX
What's an Azusa Street?

"O LORD revive your work in the midst of the years!" Habakkuk 3:2

While browsing through the shelves of a local church's bookstore, a book fell off the shelf and landed at my feet. Picking it up, I read the title "Azusa Street," written by Frank Bartleman.

I said to my friend, "What's an Azusa Street?"

She shrugged her shoulders and said, "I have no clue. Why don't you check it out then you can tell me?"

"OK! I will."

I had no idea how long and how far that journey was going to take me, but the Holy Spirit did. It all began with the reading of Bartleman's book, which chronicled the mighty revival of God's power through the Holy Spirit in a tiny horse stable in Los Angeles, California in the early 1900's. During this revival, hungry saints and sinners of all races and all nations came from all over the world to be filled with God's Word and His Holy Spirit baptism.

Bartleman's account of the revival supernaturally awakened a hunger and thirst inside me for a deeper experience with Father God. Remember, I said earlier that I can't get enough of God, and I always want more. Once you experience Him, you will understand why. I read that book many times and found myself growing discontented with "Professional Christianity" that I encountered in most churches. I cried out to God for more, more, and more of the real true God in a church fellowship like they had at Azusa Street.

"Where is it, Lord?" I humbly asked.

After that revelation, while helping to minister God's love and grace in a skid-row mission in downtown Los Angeles, I questioned the pastor of the mission about Azusa Street. He knew all about it and shared with me the exact location of the famous Azusa street.

"The old mission isn't there anymore," he observed. "But the street is. You go down this road to

Spring Street and make a left then a quick right and drive real slow. Don't blink because if you do, you'll miss it," he instructed.

I followed his directions and found the narrow, faded cobblestone street that was only wide enough for one automobile. I parked my car and walked the street where mighty Christian believers walked so long ago as part of the historic Pentecostal Movement. I felt chills run down my arms as I considered the significance of this place.

About a week later, my friend and I returned to Azusa Street to walk and pray. After a few moments, we heard loud moans, which we discovered upon closer inspection were coming from a disheveled man; a wounded, sick soul crouched behind some rubbish cans. Cautiously approaching him, we got a glimpse of his matted hair and alcohol-induced red face shinning with sweat. His dirty, once blue overalls spotted with axle grease hung off of his body when he pulled himself up with his weathered hands with gnarled knuckles and tried to grab a nearby pole. That's when the reek of old accumulated perspiration filled the air around him with repugnant fumes that made us gasp for a second. However, we were not fearful or distracted by his foul odor. Our only concern was to get help from some workers in the area to take him to

the Union Rescue Mission. We knew he could receive
all the attention that he required for his body as well
as his soul there. God is awesome. He will meet your
needs wherever you are.

Later that year, I was honored to meet veteran
Christian journalist Thomas Nickel, former editor of
Testimony magazine. An article on Azusa Street, which
appeared in the magazine, prompted me to write and
question him about William Seymour, the founder of
the Azusa Mission. Nickel also authored a book about
the revival, *Azusa Street Outpouring.* In addition, he
published the *Full Gospel Men's Voice* a publication of
the *Full Gospel Business Men's Fellowship,* also birthed out
of the Azusa revival. Father God knows how to
connect the dots. He is the original "networker."

The information I received about Seymour led me
to the house where the believers held meetings before
they moved to Azusa Street. I strolled through the
doorway of 216 Bonnie Brae Street where the revival
outpouring began and saw most of the old, original
furnishings. I also met Mrs. Simms inside, the woman
who now lived in the house. She invited me to join her
and others in prayer. I accepted with a humble heart.

Soon after that, I received a note from Brother
Nickel, and he asked if I would join with him and
David du Plessis (Mr. Pentecost), in planning and

organizing the 80ᵗʰ anniversary celebration of Azusa Street, which would be held in Pasadena, California. Look at God! Of course, I said, "Yes" and I was again humbled by his invitation.

After all of those exciting years, I thought my Azusa Street experience was fulfilled. However, it appears that it is not over, because here I am writing this historical memoir for you. I give Father God all of the praise and all of the glory due His holy name for saving my life, my mind, and giving me the precious gift of eternal life.

Food for Thought...

Curiosity to explore the unknown and seek truth often opens new doors of wisdom. God inspires curiosity through His creativity.

- When did you use curiosity to discover truth and wisdom?

- How does the Word of God ignite your curiosity?

- While curiosity can lead people down paths that do not honor God, it can also lead us to seek for God. Can you think of an illustration in the Bible where curiosity led someone to encounter God?

- Consider the words in Jeremiah 29:13. How has curiosity helped you to seek after God?

And ye shall seek me and find me when ye
shall search for me with all your heart.
Jeremiah 29:13

Chapter X

Musings on the Freedom of Aging:
It Is Time to Put the Oil in the Lamps.

"Watch therefore: for ye know not what hour
your Lord doth come." Matthew 24:42

A strange thing happened to me on the way to growing old; I sometimes struggle with being patient. I no longer care about being politically correct. I feel as if I don't have time to be considerate of inconsiderate people. The eternity clock is ticking downward, and my days on planet earth are numbered. I feel free from self-imposed restraints of being tolerant of other's frivolous views. Competing has given way to the urgency of finishing my many half-started projects. And I am determined to finish this Christian race well.

Satan has lost! Father God and I are in control of my mind. Therefore, I now carefully guard my thoughts and refuse entry to any that are not aligned with truth.

For now, this period of old age seems to last much longer than the period of my youth, which I find strange, because I thought in my youth that I would never mature. However, to those groping to be correct in their life-game, I say, "Wake-up, the Christian life is exciting and new; a refreshing exhilaration to the aging soul."

Quality time, savored time, allotted time has become my most precious commodity. No amount of money can buy me anymore time. When it is gone, it is over, done, finished. The heavy weight of material things steals time by the attention they demand. I'm shedding things. Watches, jewelry, clothes, shoes, clutter, clutter, clutter, and all things unnecessary in bringing my journey to a successful, meaningful, spiritual end must go.

Over the years, I've learned that Father God is in everything. Everything comes from Him, and He turns everything around for my good. He has a specific purpose for all my adversity. He uses all my pains, sufferings, and hardships to "grow me up" and teach me about His goodness and faithfulness. Therefore, I can rejoice in Him and how He is making all the "crooked things" straight in my life.

As a result, society's current events hold no interest in the light of a new dawning with Christ. It seems that all of these events have taken place before, only the names have changed. My soul awakens to the ticking-clock. I savor life's majestic moments by recalling and unlocking memories trapped in time. What a curse it is to be frozen in the past; unable to ascend to the next moment beyond the veil. Triviality is becoming less and less desirable as I frolic in the present and dabble in the future. The time comes when I would like to sit and wait for the final trumpet call, but that would be an ineffectual luxury that I cannot afford to entertain while lost souls are perishing. Movement is the order of the day; rest is the sanctuary of the night. Sleep, blessed sleep, draws the curtain until another dawn peeks through, kissing my cheek again.

Therefore, this race, my race, must be finished with quality and won with perseverance. I will not exit a loser. I now refuse to maintain an attitude of defeatism. By God's grace, I will gratefully close my eyes with dignity at His appointed time, fully expecting to awaken again in His Holy presence.

I have noticed lately amid the noise and clatter of this present world there is an eerie stillness, which hovers above earth's confusion. Engulfed in an aura of the supernatural, a gentle breath of wind prevails, stirring the trees to wave their limbs in praise. "Hosanna, Hosanna, to the King of Kings," their branches sing in perfect harmony.

An awesome apprehension of a sudden climatic earthshaking event surrounds nature's stillness.

Shhh! Quiet my soul. Sit in silence and listen to the voice of the trees. Close your eyes and meditate on His holiness and purity.

Now, consider the parable of the ten virgins. Five of them were not ready to go when the bridegroom (Jesus) called, because they were without the necessary oil for their lamps. That precious oil is the abiding presence of the Holy Spirit who fills our spiritual lamps. Oh, how I pray to be spiritually ready when Jesus comes. I pray He will find me with enough oil to make the trip with Him.

Therefore, I will not call this the last chapter or the end because I have many chapters yet to be written by His mighty hand in mine.

Food for Thought...

I give thanks to God that I do not have some vague indefinite future. I am grateful that His plan for my life was laid out from the beginning of time and that I was able to hear His voice and follow the path.

- Have you accepted the truth that God has a path for your life?
- How do you think your God-ordained path will give you a joyous future?
- How can your chosen path help others?
- How will your influence give light to generations to come?
- Consider the words of Psalm 16:11.

Thou wilt show me the path of life. In Thy presence is fullness of joy. At Thy right hand, there are pleasures forevermore.
Psalm 16:11

I met the author of *The True Azusa Street Story*, Thomas R. Nickel.

A Letter to the Readers

Dear Reader:

If you should die today, where would you spend eternity? God tells us in His word, "And it is appointed unto men once to die, but after this, the judgment" (Hebrews 9:27).

Since death is certain, you must prepare to meet God. According to God's Word, you will spend eternity in one of two places—either heaven or hell. Here is the good news of the Gospel. In spite of your sin, God loves you and has done everything necessary for your salvation. Pray this simple prayer and mean it with all your heart.

"Dear Lord, I know that I am a sinner, but I am sorry for my sins. I believe the Lord Jesus died for me, shed His precious blood for me and rose again, and with all my heart I turn from my sin and receive Him as my Savior right now. Thank you, LORD, for saving me! Amen.

For more information contact:
The Fellowship Tract League
P.O. Box 164, Lebanon, Ohio 45036
www.fellowshiptractleague.org tract # 167

APPENDIX

The World Health Organization report for suicide dated May 2017 states:

Over 800,000 people die due to suicide every year and ten to twenty times more people attempted suicide worldwide. This on average, is one death every forty seconds and one attempt every three seconds.

Suicide is the second leading cause of death among people who are fifteen to twenty-nine-years-old.

Seventy-five percent of global suicides occur in low and middle-income countries.

Non-fatal attempted suicides are also a concern. More than 3,700 youths were hospitalized after attempting suicide. Sixty-six percent of the hospitalizations happened to female youths.

For more information, visit the World Health Organization's website at http://www.who.int.

About the Author

Marlene E. Kelly is a retired educator and a freelance writer living in Atlanta, Georgia. She writes magazine articles and short stories for numerous publications, including *Trusting Him When Life's Difficult* (Create Space, 2016), *Trusting Him When Life's Messy* (Create Space, 2016), *Miracles & Moments of Grace* (Createspace, 2013), *I believe in Heaven* (Regal, 2013), *Trusting Him with Your Addicted Child* (Create Space, 2013) *Skinned Knees and Skate Keys* (Jawbone, 2010), and *Count It All Joy* (Jawbone, 2009). In addition, she has served as a ghostwriter and copy-editor for numerous books.

Marlene is an alumna of UC Cincinnati with a Masters of Education; Fuller Theological Seminary-School of World Missions, and William Carey International University in Pasadena, California. In addition, she has served as a State Representative for Christian Educators International in Ohio.

mk082892@aol.com; mk93707@gmail.com

MEKelly-SolidRock.blogspot.com

More Books from Greentree Publishers

For more information on these titles, visit our website at www.greentreepublishers.com

Immovable: Standing Firm in the Last Days

By Tim Riordan

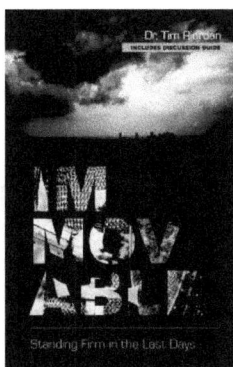

Does Bible prophecy indicate that we are living in the last days? What should Christians do to be ready for the days ahead? Dr. Tim Riordan shares biblical truths on Bible prophecy and how the Church can stand firm in the last days. Through a careful study of Bible prophecy related to the last days, Dr. Riordan shows the connection between the spiritual armor of Ephesians 6 and the spiritual warfare that will take place in the days leading up to Christ's return. This book also offers a small group discussion guide. You can find more information about this book on Dr. Tim Riordan's website at www.timriordan.me or from www.greentreepublishers.com. It is available in paperback and e-book formats.

Songs from the Heart: Meeting with God in the Psalms

By Tim Riordan

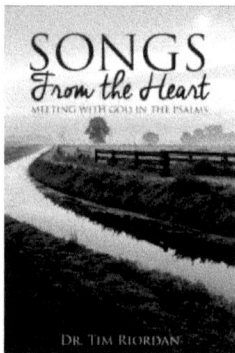

Songs from the Heart: Meeting with God in the Psalms is a Bible study/ devotional on one of the most loved books of the Bible: the Psalms. Join Dr. Tim Riordan as he shares insights on these beloved passages through Bible teaching and storytelling, making personal application to your life. This book is available in paperback and e-book formats.

The Published Pastor Series – By Tim Riordan

Book One – Expanding Your Ministry Through Writing and Publishing

Book Two – How to Write and Publish Books

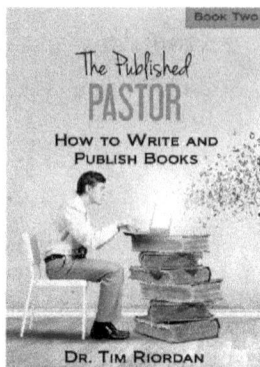

Would you like to expand your ministry by turning your next sermon series into a book your congregation can pass on to others? *The Published Pastor* series is a collection of books that will encourage you to write and offer you the step-by-step help you may need to become a published author. This series will eventually include 3 books that will be a valuable resource for any aspiring writer. This series is available as individual digital books or you can choose Books 1 & 2 in a combined paperback.

Reaching for Life
By Victoria Teague with Connie J. Singleton

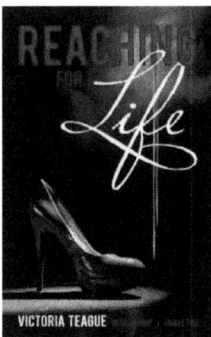

Following an eleven-year cocaine addiction and a dangerous career as a dancer in Atlanta's sex industry, Victoria Teague experienced what can only be called a miraculous rescue. For ten years after she left the clubs, she sat respectably in the pews of her church with a grateful heart and a zip-locked mouth. She built an entirely new life on top of embarrassing secrets from her past, and only a precious, trusted few knew her spiritual rags-to-riches story. That is until one ordinary day when she was asked to do anything *but* the ordinary. On that day, she was called not only to share her secrets, but also to spotlight them. To use them as her "street cred" to minister to other women in the strip clubs who desperately need a lifeline like the one she was offered. To seek the lost and give them hope for a better life. Available in paperback and e-book formats from your favorite retailer.

www.ingramcontent.com/pod-product-compliance
Lightning Source LLC
Chambersburg PA
CBHW071828020426
42331CB00007B/1648